RESCUE OF A GARDEN

RESCUE OF A GARDEN

Restoring a Lost Garden in Brundall, Norfolk

Janet Muter

HALSGROVE

# Acknowledgements

The list of people who have helped with the restoration of Brundall Gardens is endless. From the gardeners who unearthed the bones of the original gardens, to the friends who taught me so much about gardening.

When I started to write this book I asked Beth Chatto if she thought it a good idea to include advice on the many ways of reducing work in the garden and she kindly wrote some helpful notes on my original script.

My thanks go also to Doreen Normandale, for help with the nomenclature of the plants.

Much of the history of the garden has been provided by the family of the original owners who bequeathed me so many relative memoirs and documents.

Without my daughter Rosalind's help to incorporate the photos into the script, a job far beyond my capabilities this book would never have been written.

First published in Great Britain in 2015
Copyright © 2015 Janet Muter and Rosalind Painting

British Library Cataloguing-in-Publication Data
A CIP record for this title is available from the British Library

ISBN 978 0 85704 259 0

HALSGROVE
Halsgrove House, Ryelands Business Park,
Bagley Road, Wellington, Somerset TA21 9PZ
Tel: 01823 653777   Fax: 01823 216796
email: sales@halsgrove.com

Part of the Halsgrove group of companies
Information on all Halsgrove titles is available at:
www.halsgrove.com

Printed in China by Everbest Printing Co Ltd

Contents

A dream waiting to be fulfilled; Brundall Gardens 1984

🌸 Introduction

On a rather overcast spring afternoon in 1984 I drove with my mother from our neighbouring village of Great Plumstead to shop in Brundall, a riverside village east of Norwich. The gardens were full of spring flowers and blossom, something we missed in our isolated country house. As we drove into the village I noticed a road sign which read 'Lake View Drive'. Idly wondering what Lake it might be, I turned into the road and was confronted by two large houses under construction. As there was no sign of activity we investigated further and saw, falling away from the buildings a steep valley, and sheltering under a great forest of trees three ponds leading down to the shores of a lake. The land was totally overgrown, but I saw a garden just waiting to be reclaimed!

Janet Muter

Lake House 1986

A House Undressed

Ayear later, our extended family had outgrown our home in Great Plumstead and Garry, my husband, and I were looking for a new home which could also accommodate my mother when she needed some care.

Lake House, 1986. A house undressed.

One morning Garry opened the paper and there in the house sales advertisements page was a picture, not of a house, but of the garden that I had not forgotten since I had last seen it on that Spring afternoon. There was a house too, a house that would provide exactly the accommodation we would need for visiting grandchildren and a flat for my mother.

The land was not so simple, as the owners of one of the houses overlooking the valley, already owned the middle pond. The landowner eventually gave us a further two acres of land to the west of the house when his planning permission was withdrawn. It would only have cost him money to maintain it as it bore a covenant to be kept weed free. They jested, of course.

When the houses were built a conservation order had been imposed, and the area declared a site of natural beauty in an endeavour to save what had once

The trees that had to go …

… To let the garden flow

The dream fulfilled

been one of the most spectacular horticultural creations in Norfolk – Brundall Gardens.

When we moved in, our neighbour's first comment was "I hope you're going to remove those trees", not the forest trees you understand, but a row of conifers defining our border line. We were delighted that they, like us, envisaged the gardens flowing seamlessly together in this lovely valley.

However, I realised that at the age of 57, if I wanted to manage this large area for a number of years, I would need to aim for maximum effect with minimum effort. The gardens had become a wonderful habitat for wildlife. Woodlands, water and hedgerow birds were all here; and amphibians and insect life had adopted this undisturbed place.

Hazel Corylus tortuosa *creates an effective sculpture, standing alone on a bed of chipped bark*

Mallard ducklings in their nest by the bottom pond

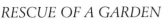

*The rhododendrons had survived
the invasion of bracken*

*The many shades of granny's bonnets
Aquilegia seed around but are easily
controlled and die gracefully*

Opposite: Divided annually these snowdrops turn winter into spring

All my planting, therefore, would be to add to nature's bounty with berry-bearing shrubs and small trees and self-seeding native flowers in abundance. It was, however, necessary first to be able to move around in it.

Dog daisies just arrived on the grass bank years ago and take over in June

Cyclamen hederifolium *and* coum *have colonised the woods under the holm oak*

Adrian Thomas, our neighbour, had carved out some paths giving access to the lake in the year before we moved in. He also made a path round the lake. Before Alan Jones acquired the rest of the garden in 2000, i.e. the lake and its environs, we had tried to arrest the worst of the dereliction by killing the bracken, rescuing shrubs and trees and keeping paths open. There were steps hidden under years of leaf mould and an ever-invading stand of Polygonum and Indian balsam. For fifteen years we gave the area as much maintenance as we could but we were more than a little delighted when Alan and his team moved in.

Right: Alders on the lake edge
Below: After their removal

PART ONE
A History of the Garden

Dr Beverley

'Brundall Gardens' was the brain child of one Michael Beverley. He was born in Brooke in Norfolk in 1841, the only son of Michael and Mary Anne Beverley, who were servants at Brooke House. He attended the village school and, showing exceptional ability, was sent as a boarder to Bracondale School in Norwich. At 15 he was very fortunate to be apprenticed to Dr William Bransby Francis with whom he lodged. Dr and Mrs Francis were very kind to him, treating him as a son and it was from Dr Francis that he learned his photographic skills, to which we are indebted for his later pictures of the garden. Dr Francis was the 'Poor Law' doctor for Costessey where typhus was endemic. Michael learned how to vaccinate babies against small pox, a rare disease now but one of which he was to have experience later. He progressed from being an assistant to witnessing operations and then becoming a dresser to the senior surgeon and a clinical clerk at the Norfolk and Norwich Hospital. All this at a fascinating time for him to be training. James Simpson was introducing chloroform to the profession, and Lister antiseptics. Michael was in his late teens while all this was happening. In London he was appointed dresser to Sir William Ferguson at King's College. He obtained his degree of M.D. before the legal age of 21, but it seems no one asked him his age!

This enabled him to spend a year in Paris before he could practise, studying, and, as his grandmother comments in her memoirs, 'and have a great deal of fun'. But he did work, learning practical surgery and the special skills

Opposite: After the Second World War

Dr Michael Beverley

required to be a paediatrician. He worked with the great and the good, but also applied himself to the lowlier need for decent sanitation in schools.

He was a devotee of the theatre and enjoyed ice skating on the frozen lake in the Bois de Boulogne. It was the winter of 1864 and one of the coldest. These halcyon days were abruptly ended when he had to return home to earn a living. The house surgery post of the Norfolk and Norwich Hospital was vacant due to the resignation of Mr Williams and Michael applied for, and was awarded, the post and started work on December 28th 1864. He was only 23. It was the start of his official connection to the Norfolk and Norwich Hospital, which lasted some forty years.

He began to employ trained nurses from the Florence Nightingale School at St Thomas' and settled the retiring unqualified nurses in the Great Hospital. He introduced a more informal atmosphere to the Norfolk and Norwich Hospital, with more visitors, and at Christmas even a decorated tree.

It was about this time that there was an epidemic of small pox in Norwich and the first isolation hospital was built. Dr Michael was sent as its medical officer. He was very experienced in this field of medicine. His years of training had given him an unusual gift for diagnosis in many areas of medicine and his opinion was widely sought.

In 1873, aged 32, he married Marian (Polly) Hotblack, 23, the eldest daughter of John Hotblack, a shoe manufacturer. They had six surviving children, and lived in a comfortable house in Norwich, spending their holidays in a rented house in Overstrand.

It was in 1881 that Dr Beverly started a new hobby. He had always had an interest in botany, but, unlike many amateur botanists who potter around the lanes in tweed hats with a magnifying glass, he bought seventy-six acres of farmland in Brundall on the banks of the River Yare. It was bounded on the north side by a steep escarpment and divided by the relatively new railway line to the south. A deep cleft in the escarpment inspired him to build a line of four ponds. They varied in depth from two to four feet, and were lined with brick and concrete, much of which still remains in good condition to this

The east wood

day. They were separated by four-foot high rockeries, through which the springs that fed them flowed down to the lake. When I started to uncover these rockeries I marvelled at the tons of carrstone required to build them, all brought presumably by horse and cart from West Norfolk.

In the process of digging out and lining his large ponds, Dr Beverley found Roman artefacts and remains which included some that, after careful scrutiny and deliberation by the archaeologist Cyril Fox, indicated the possibility of Roman boat-building and boat repairing activities in the 'Dock'. This surely pointed to the existence of a Roman villa above, certainly to a Roman presence of some kind. Probably no one will ever know whether the buried nails and fragments of wood in the clay indicate boat-building or not. Subsequent study of the configuration of the nearby River Yare at that time by Eric Cooper, incline him to the view that they do. In truth it does not much matter. This is undoubtedly Roman territory. They were here, as were the Saxons at a later date. So, in this way did this spectacular cleft in the hillside acquire its name, 'Roman Dock'.

The other spectacular feature of Brundall Gardens is its abundance of specimen trees. Established as they are now, and towering at heights of nearly ninety feet above the slopes of the Dock and the lily lake below, it required a quite deliberate act of imagination to realise the vision this remarkable man must have had of an almost unique arboretum of oaks and cedars, beeches, yew and ash. The weeping trees are especially fine. Sadly the weeping ash, a truly architectural tree, was a casualty of the 2013 gales. I am going to make it into a sculpture, planted with some of the many different ferns I have introduced to the garden over the years. They love the shady slopes and moist air beneath the trees.

The ponds before they became overshadowed by trees

The ponds are shaded now by forest trees 100 years old

Varieties of Polystichum *which keep their leaves in winter*

October 1987. The Great Storm

The new jetty

May in paradise

The Lake

The lake itself is much as it was in Dr Beverley's time, except that the water lilies he planted have increased into large floating islands of flowers. The plants came from Joseph Bory Latour Marliac. The story of how he finally came to hybridise them is told in a paper by Kit Knott who tells us the great breakthrough came when *Nymphaea odorata* 'Rosea' was finally sent to Marliac from the USA. The doyen of American horticulturists, one Mr Hovey, had been persuaded by a Godfrey le Boeuf to try to obtain it from his neighbour in whose hands was the monopoly of this plant. The neighbour was adamant about refusing to part with his plant until Marliac sent one thousand francs to lay on the table. Marliac got his plant. From this plant were bred all the different pink and red water lilies we see in our parks and gardens today.

The lake circa 1900

Fishing competition circa 1900

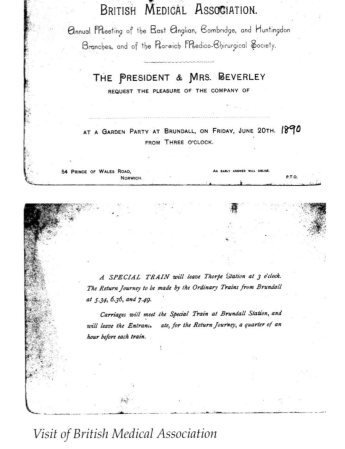

Visit of British Medical Association

They make Brundall mere, as it has come to be called, a very special place. It was stocked, and still is, with a variety of fish, some wild, some introduced. Dr Beverley bred trout in the ponds for the enjoyment of his friends at his fishing parties. There were other parties we know for friends and family. He hosted the annual meeting of the BMA in Norwich in June 1890 and his wife invited those attending to a party in the gardens. It is evident from family records that he enjoyed sharing his creation with whoever cared to see it.

He recorded much of what he grew here. Such things as eucalyptus, yucca and cordyline were deemed tender and probably were at that time. Records of skating on the lake tell us that the winters must have been colder then. Since we have lived here, only once in the winter of 1985/6 has the lake frozen hard enough to bear the weight of a skater. I may have skated on thin ice since then, but not on Brundall mere!

An evergreen winter border...

...and in flower in summer

Yuccas in the snow

Dr Beverley frequently went abroad to attend medical conferences and returned with plants he had found for his collection. The number of specimen trees increased, a chusan palm still shelters in the woods, and he had a collection of hollies, now readily available from specialist growers but rare at that time. I have added acers to grow in the shelter of the trees, and azaleas and rhododendrons which thrive. If well mulched they are little trouble, considering the explosion of colour and scent they provide.

Below and overleaf:
Japanese azaleas loving
the Broadland peat

Rhododendron 'Cunningham'

Rhododendron 'Lemon Ice'

Rhododendron 'Silver Slipper'
Bought for their scent
while in Cumbria

Rhododendron
Coccinea Speciosar

Walking through the woods towards the eastern end of the lake one can still see the remains of what were once farmworkers' cottages. Dr Beverley converted one of them into a museum to house the collection of rare pottery that had been discovered during the excavation of the ponds. He made a wishing well and designed a fountain: gravity powered. Clever stuff. The present one is powered by electricity, but is large enough to make a rainbow on a sunny day. It oxygenates the pond and is a deterrent to the ever-threatening blanket weed.

The wishing well

With the trees and the shrubs came the birds. Water fowl adapted to the open water of the mere and the marsh. Dr Beverley was a founder member of the Norfolk Naturalists' Trust, now the Norfolk Wildlife Trust.

Here ends all I think I need to say about the influence of Dr Beverley on my part in the restoration of Brundall Gardens. He retired from his work at the Norfolk and Norwich Hospital in 1911, moving to Scole, near Diss. At about this time he sold some of the land for building plots. Little is known of what happened at Brundall Gardens from this time until he sold the rest of the estate in 1919 to Frederick Holmes Cooper. Presumably they were maintained through the years of the First World War and used for holidays by the family.

The museum

Frederick Holmes Cooper

Frederick Cooper was a self-made man whose career in the emergent cinema industry has been well documented in Stephen Peart's book *The Picture House in East Anglia*. He and his wife and two sons, Eric and Ashley, moved into the Log House, a substantially built family home, which he added to and lavishly embellished. He set about making the Gardens into a great visitor attraction. Unfortunately, on 13th November of that year, a fire broke out in the Log House at about 7 p.m. The *Eastern Daily Press* described what happened in the next day's newspaper, 19th November 1919:

"Considerable excitement was caused in Brundall and District last evening when the Log House, well known to railway travellers and in the occupation of Mr F.H. Cooper, was totally destroyed by fire. It is understood that the outbreak started in the roof, the first intimation that something was amiss was a strong smell of burning. The Norwich Fire Brigade was summoned by telephone. The house, constructed entirely of wood with a thatched roof, was however an early prey to the flames and the situation made it impossible for anything to be done prior to the arrival of the Brigade. People meanwhile had not been slow to notice the signs of the conflagration in the sky and a crowd assembled. The flames rapidly increased their hold and darted up to a great height, being accompanied by clouds of smoke and showers of sparks. Upon their arrival the Brigade speedily got to work, the engine drawing the copious supply from the ornamental water in the grounds, but they were unable to do much and it was impossible to save even the furniture owing to the doors being locked. They, however, stuck manfully to the task. A relief force was detached from Norwich at about 11.00 p.m. and some of the original Brigade were enabled to return home, but at midnight the engine was still engaged at the scene of the outbreak."

Brundall Log House following the fire of 1919

The hotel before and after its demise

"Mr Cooper is of the opinion that the fire must have had its origin in an indoor beam. The moral resolve that he has drawn from the calamity is that he will live in no more wooden houses as long as he lives. Pitch pine may be all very well for a coffin or for pews in church. His preference for the future will lie with bricks and mortar."

Undeterred, he replaced the Log House with the impressive three-storey Redclyffe House overlooking the mere and the River Yare. He arranged for better access to the Gardens, persuading the L.N.E.R. to build a Halt, Brundall Gardens railway station, bringing visitors from Norwich virtually to his gate. He also founded the Brundall Gardens Steamship Company, and its brochure enthusiastically described the trip up the river from Yarmouth.

Redclyffe House in the 1920s

He built a tea-shop and then a hotel on the river bank. Sadly the foundations of the hotel were built on peat, and it eventually broke its back, the ruins left until it was struck by lightning. The tea-shop still stands, half flooded.

At the time, however, people flocked to see this amazing place in their thousands, 60,000 we are told in 1922. Unlike Dr Beverley, Frederick Cooper was not a plantsman or a horticulturist, but he recognised this, and delegated the garden management to the head gardener, Strachan, who, Frederick Cooper's son Eric, describes as having exceptional talent. It was Eric Cooper who was in charge of the management of the mere. When he and his niece, Caroline Seville, Ashley Cooper's daughter, visited us in 1987, he gave me a detailed description of his duties. With some I agreed. Certainly the alders needed and still need to be kept well away from the edge of the mere, and the detritus which the prevailing wind always seems to blow on to my little beach needs removing. But trapping the water voles? Never! Nor do I cut back all of the reeds and rushes in which the water birds nest. I think Frederick Cooper liked to keep things tidy, not always conducive to wildlife gardening and would not have thought much of my patches of stinging nettles. I do cut

The steamship outside the tea rooms in the 1930s

Opposite: Reeds and rushes fluffy in the March wind
Photo: Philip Harston

them back before they seed, allowing another flush of young leaves for the caterpillars. My grandmother, from whom I learned my love of gardens, always had a rough patch of grass at the end of hers where buttercups, miniature daffodils and fritillaries grew, and there were frogs which made me jump.

The Stringer Family

When the cinema business suffered a decline in the nineteen thirties, Frederick Cooper became ill, and having built thirty-six bungalows on his land to the west of the estate, sold the rest of it to the Stringer family for their private use. They were not, however, to enjoy their new home for long. The army requisitioned Redclyffe House as an enemy aircraft plotting station and they had to move out.

In July 1993 we had a visit from a Gladys Vincent and her friend Sally. She said they were attached to the 69th S/L Regiment, Royal Fusiliers, with Colonel William Kenyon and Major J.B. William from 1941–43. Their ATS Commander was a Miss Chattey, all three from London. She said the visit brought back a lot of memories, and although wartime discipline was strict, they all accepted it and loved the house and garden. She said she is still in touch with two of her other mates.

Doreen Oliver continues the story:

> *"ATS plotter G.M. Croswell (neé Bussey) said that she had remembered visiting the Gardens in the Cooper's time and was delighted when she learned that she was to be billeted there. She described the ground floor of the house with the officers' Mess and sitting room and the switchboard where she worked. Officers slept upstairs and the plotters were housed in a cottage in the grounds, with the battery office in the pre-war tea-room. They enjoyed tennis and swimming in the ponds, though boating on the lake was banned following a few pranks and after-dark liaisons."*

Michael Aspen

Only one elderly gardener was retained and so it must have been quite a task for the Stringers to restore the place to its former glory when they finally returned in 1945. They enjoyed a time of peace and privacy until 1968 when they sold the house and the remaining eighteen acres of land to Michael Aspen, a property developer. Aspen applied to the local council to build sixty-two houses, mainly above and round the lake, but there were endless delays.

The grounds once more became overgrown and to the concern of the local inhabitants, gypsies moved in and some of the trees were damaged.

J.W. Cousins & Sons

In 1969 the beautiful Redclyffe House burned down. Finally, after two attempts to develop the area during which the developers went into receivership, J.W. Cousins & Sons acquired the land and in 1984/5 built two houses, Mr and Mrs Thomas's and ours. At last peace and harmony had returned to Brundall Gardens. Peter Cousins' son was a school friend of our son and our relationship was always cordial. Even before we acquired the adjacent overgrown land from him, I was allowed a fairly free hand. We reduced the closely-planted beech hedge which separates the garden from the road to a manageable eight feet in height. As it keeps its lovely bronze leaves all the winter, it provides all year round cover and nesting sites for a variety of birds. One annual cut in late July suffices. I planted small native woodland trees in the grassed area at the western end of the garden and under-planted them with spring bulbs.

No wild garden is complete without foxgloves, loved by bees and cross pollinated give many shades of colour

Winter wonderland in the woods

Even a modern shed may take on a rustic air if surrounded by early May flowers

🌸 PART TWO
My Rescue of the Garden

When we officially acquired the extra land, I planted the slope near the road with the ever-accommodating *Geranium macrorrhizum*, perennial wallflowers, and hebes. The steps which lead from here to my wooden shed, are edged with cotinus and a charming *Lonicera syringantha* which, like all the honeysuckles, smells delicious. The shed itself is host to another honeysuckle, 'Halliana', a rose and a clematis. Many different buddleias have seeded around in this area, adding interest and benefiting the butterflies which feed on them. Dead-headed from time to time they will continue flowering into the autumn. The Sorbus family of trees can provide a variety of coloured berries, not just the familiar red of the mountain ash among them, but also 'Joseph Rock' with golden berries and 'Kashmiriana' with pinkish white. I mentioned small native trees planted on the edge of the larger woodland specimens, but among these are also young pines, a bay and a maple, which when grown to maturity will add to the height and density of the wood. The smaller trees include field maple and a spindle, *Euonymous europaeus*, which provide brilliant autumn colour.

An unusual hawthorn *Crataegeus prunifolia* 'Rosea' is quite a tall tree and its berries are a spectacular crimson red. Too many to mention, these trees and shrubs grow in their own deep leaf litter from which emerge in spring, bluebells, campion, stitchwort and self-seeded forget-me-nots, descendent of a rich blue one that my mother grew. Brambles, lamium, herb robert and other over-zealous woodlanders will also compete if allowed to do so, but are easy enough to pull out of the soft ground if caught early. A five-stemmed bramble pretending to be a rose, one good pull and it's out. Very satisfying. Keeping a regular and watchful eye on any emerging weeds can be a relatively easy way to maintain a lovely woodland garden.

*Narcissus follow
snowdrops and give
way to campion and
bluebells at the
wood's edge*

How tidy one should be in a garden, what to remove and what to leave is one of the most difficult things to get right. I leave seedheads for the birds in autumn and only cut back herbaceous growth in the early spring when the bulbs have emerged. Heavily mulched with chipped bark, the ground does not become so easily compacted.

The only flat area of the garden where I could plan to have a bed of herbaceous plants, was a grassed area on the north side of two great forest trees, a holm oak and a sweet chestnut. The soil was solid clay. I scrounged

'Bressingham Pink' is a magnificent buddleia with huge racemes or flowers, but I think the butterflies prefer the heavily scented blue varieties

The same border in spring and in summer

Anemone japonica *and* Sedum spectabile

compost from everyone and anyone and we incorporated it into this seemingly hostile environment and created a reasonably fertile island bed. I chose my plants with care bearing in mind what had done well in a similar situation in my previous garden. I planted Japanese anemones and astrantias in the deepest shade, and further forward in the bed, campanulas in variety according to their height. I added pulmonarias and bergenias for winter interest, and gave the bed a backbone with cornus and cotinus. Cyclamen grow prolifically under the holm oak seeding freely in its rich leaf mould, and *Helleborus orientalis* and the small white narcissus 'Jenny' survive the onslaught of sweet chestnuts in the autumn. For some reason all these plants are pest free, and I wonder what I am doing, or not doing, to maintain this happy state of affairs. Unless, of course, you include slugs as pests, and I

Helleborus orientalis *and narcissus 'Jenny' in early March*

guess if you grow seedlings you should. I thought cosmos and nicotiana (tobacco plants) would enhance the bed. I should have taken my own advice and stuck to perennials. The replacement aster nova belgii do very well, as do mallows.

Ground Cover

When Garry and I first came here in 1985 there were very few flowers in the leafy wood, but the brambles and the more aggressive weeds have largely been cleared to make way for native species. Snowdrops and bluebells have increased year by year in the deep leaf litter under the oaks. Primroses fill every sunny spot that they can find.

Rhododendron 'Lemon Ice' and choisya 'Sundance' make a brilliant impact on a shady slope

Primroses self seed and bloom from February to May

Bordering this woodland area I have introduced variegated ivies to give winter colour, and shrubs to compliment them such as euonymous and choisya 'Sundance'. The leaves of this lovely shrub appear to have been varnished when touched by the sun. Shrubs are fairly easy to maintain and I have planted many of them throughout the garden. Underplanted with carefully chosen perennials and properly mulched, they create impact without too much work.

Opposite: Borders packed with shrubs and ground-covering geraniums

Geraniums, "Sue Crug", "Patrick" and "Lasting Impression"

Hardy Geraniums

I think I should mention here some of the most effective plants to grow under, among, and even over shrubs. I suppose that my first introduction to the hardy geranium family of plants was when I bought a plant of *Geranium endressii* 'Wargrave Pink'. It reproduced itself prolifically and by division I had soon edged my border with this dainty silvery pink and long-flowering plant. That was in another life when I had a very large and formal garden. Here at Lake House, I have a very large and *informal* garden, with a variety of habitats and for each one there is a geranium to suit it. The first to provide a flash of colour in spring does so, not with its flowers, but with its wonderful primrose-yellow leaves, scrolled with red like other phaeum varieties. It was a seedling I found in the garden and I have called it 'Brundall Gold'. The phaeums are some of the earliest to bloom with their tiny faces and colours ranging from white to very nearly black, an especially pretty one is named 'Lily Lovell', named for his mother by Trevor Bath, an author and authority on hardy geraniums.

Geranium pratense, a true blue that grows in profusion in the wild, seeds itself everywhere in my garden, even in a tree stump. Everywhere that is except where I want it to grow, in the wildflower meadow. The determination of plants to grow where they want to, and not where I want them to never fails to amaze me. There are many pratense varieties and colours, all tall and lax in habit, and therefore best grown among neighbours who will give them some support.

From small six-inch plants which have been cut back by the winter, allowing them to be interplanted with bulbs, some varieties can spread as much as a metre in the summer. Geranium 'Khan' is an example of this. The deep purple 'Patrick' sprawling among salmon pink 'Lasting Impression' or 'Rozanne' a true blue *Geranium wallichianum* tangling with 'Maderense' make a summer-long source of nectar for hungry insects. A very easy alternative to summer bedding.

I have a dry bank left where an elm met its untimely end due to Dutch Elm Disease, and six plants of *Geranium riversleanum*. 'Mavis Simpson',

Geranium wallichianum *'Rozanne'*

Geranium macrorrhizum

Geranium platypetalum

Geranium renardii

Geranium phaeum *'Lily Lovell'*

interplanted with vincas and perennial wallflowers soon made a colourful impact. Spring bulbs and *Helleborus foetidous* fill the gaps in spring. It is one of the few dry and sunny spots in the garden. I have since added rosemary, thyme and lavender. Once planted they look after themselves but a little dead-heading will only improve them.

Geranium macrorrhizum, be its flowers cerise, pink or white, will quickly become an impenetrably dense carpet of leaves, and although its flowers do not last all summer, it rewards us with rich autumn colouring. This is one of the many attractions of geraniums to me; the contribution they make to the garden for so much of the year. The tiny corms of *Geranium tuberosum*, which send up pretty little pink flowers in May, and complement the dark purple leaves, and deep blue flowers of ajuga 'Metallica', disappear altogether after they have flowered.

Geranium phaeum *'Album'*

Geranium 'Johnson's Blue'

Geranium maculatum
'Beth Chatto'

Geranium clarkei
'Kashmir Pink'

Geranium sanguineum *'Glen Luce'*

Geranium himalayense *'Gravetye'*

Geranium sanguineum *'Elke'*

Geranium macrorrhizum
Ingwersen's Variety'

Many of the oxonianum varieties will grow in dense shade in the woods but their colours appear less strong. Very promiscuous and seeding freely, it is wise to dead-head them after flowering. If they have formed a carpet, this may be done with a strimmer.

The most rampant of all the geraniums in this garden is *Geranium procurrens*. Not a subject for a small garden, but left as mine is to edge a pond, or clamber over *Choisya ternate* 'Sundance' with its black-eyed purple flowers, no longer sombre but shining like jewels among the glittering leaves of the choisya. I wouldn't be without it.

Other Ground Cover Plants

Pulmonarias (lungwort) are an undeservedly neglected addition to the flower border in early spring. From neat clumps of foliage emerge a great variety of flowers and variegated leaves. One of the earliest, 'Redstart', flowers in

Opposite: Ella (my cat) with geranium 'Mrs Kipple'

Pulmonaria 'Roy Davison'

March, salmon pink with lime green foliage, a lovely foil to the maroon foliage of bergenias, such as 'Eric Smith'. 'Roy Davison', a prolific grower, has clear blue flowers and silver foliage. The leaves of some of the later varieties are quite spectacular, large and silver or intricately marked, their markings making a valuable addition to the summer border. 'Munstead Blue' and 'Blue Ensign' have almost indigo flowers. Mine grow among scillas and chionodoxas under an orange berberis. Who says spring is all yellow and white? There are many varieties of these lovely plants ranging from white through to ice blue or pink. There is one, 'Saccharta', bred from the original plant known as 'soldiers and sailors' with large pink and blue flowers. Good in the border.

Pulmonarias gently increase each year and divide easily, making them good subjects for woodland planting. They prefer shade but are not fussy as long as they don't dry out. They might be grateful for a little mulch occasionally

Opposite: Pulmonaria

Pulmonaria 'Barfield Pink'

Lamium maculatum

Opposite: Pulmonaria 'Opal'

Winter flowering heathers

but like the garden favourites, hardy geraniums, they need little attention, although if they are dead-headed they will go on flowering well into the autumn.

To encourage any insects looking for nectar on warmer winter days, I have allowed butter burr, petasites, a space on a sheltered bank under a cedar, but this can be a really uncontrollable thug, so beware. It does, however, smell quite

Another Cumbrian find was this pink chervil chaerophyllum Hirsutum roseum

The dainty golden leaves of the gleditsia contrast well with the dark cordyline and hebes

delicious. Winter flowering heathers are a less frightening alternative but, unlike petasites, they like the sun.

Other good ground covering plants are the periwinkles, or vincas. *Vinca difformis*, for example, flowers prolifically from December onwards, its dainty ice-blue flowers seemingly reflecting the pale winter sky. The annual *Lunaria annua*, or honesty, seeding itself and blooming even in dense shade will make quite an impact.

Vinca difformis

Honesty

Among the deciduous trees, where the shade is less dense, I have Welsh poppies growing with ferns. These poppies which resemble our field poppies come in shades of yellow and orange, single or double, and some quite exquisitely edged in red. In spite of their fragile appearance they are quite tough, and they too seed freely. However, if a bright orange one offends you by placing itself next to a sugar pink bergenia, it's not difficult to remove. In Cumbria they even seed themselves in the slate walls. One of my favourite flowers, and quite endearing.

Welsh poppies, Mecanopsis cambrica

Deep blue flowers of the lithodora cover the wild flower bank in spring and deter any weeds

Roses

A.A. Milne wrote that if a house hadn't got a May tree it wasn't like a house at all. I guess most of us would say the same about a rose tree. There were a few roses struggling in the garden when we came here, including a rampant climber with double pink flowers growing into an old oak. It is still there. But most of us are not content with one rose tree, are we? We want hybrid teas with huge prize-winning flowers that win prizes and attract every known pest. So most of my roses scramble through trees or are freestanding shrubs in the border. 'Canary Bird' blooms in late April, Rosa 'Primula' with incense-scented dainty foliage, flowers at the same time, or nearly, with paler flowers. Forget-me-nots have self-seeded beneath them. An ever-recurring miracle. May I suggest that you visit a specialist rose grower, tell them exactly what you want and where you want to plant it and you will be well advised. Say that the plants must be disease-free and need the minimum of pruning just like my 'Canary Bird'.

Rosa 'Canary Bird'

Opposite: Rosa 'Rambling Rector'

Rosa 'Smarty'

If your roses are well mulched and planted in water-retentive soil, they shouldn't need watering. I really do enjoy dead-heading the climbers I have growing over an arch, breathing in their dreamy scent. 'Pink Perpetue' climbs up a drainpipe outside my front door, and as its name suggests, flowers all summer, charming but not rampant. Unlike 'Alberic Barbier' which needs pruning weekly if one is to be able to open the garage door, but a small price to pay for this lovely rose which repeat flowers into late autumn.

Rosa 'Compactum'

Rosa 'Compassion'

The Rockeries

When I removed seventeen years of detritus from them, I finally found the rockeries that divide the ponds in this garden, and they are an important feature of the landscaping. However, to build a rockery that looks natural is expensive. If you have one it can look good even without plants. Planted, tending it can be a hazardous business to those with problems of balance or weak ankles! An alternative is a raised bed or two, any shape or size to suit the space you want to fill, and at least a metre high. Easy to access for planting and arranging whatever plants or ornaments you choose, I suggest those which are happy in well-drained conditions, grey leaved or succulent. It can be a joy to see and smell these plants in close-up, such delights as dianthus or tiny perennial wallflowers.

The sloping rockery covered in rock roses, helianthemums, in summer, drops down to the bog garden with its dazzling show of king cups Caltha palustris *in spring and crocosmia in summer*

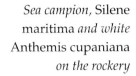

Sea campion, Silene
maritima *and white*
Anthemis cupaniana
on the rockery

A Roman pot on the rockery

The rockery in spring with gold saxifrage and blue Brunnera macrophylla *and lithodora*

The Ponds

The top pond lies at the foot of the steeply-sloping lawn but is separated from it by a shrub border and a path. We built a waterfall to cascade through the border and under the path into the pond. It wasn't difficult. We had the slope, plenty of spare carrstone, the water and access to the electricity supply which powered the fountain. I love the sound of it, as do all our guests. One of the first things that I did when we moved here was to buy myself some Musketeer water boots so that I could play in the ponds. It was a childhood dream. I filtered out lots of mud, allowing all the wee beasties to slither back into the water. There were dragonfly larvae, newts, leeches and many weird and wonderful bugs. I planted the small reed *Typha minima*, water lilies, iris and kingcups. Other plants arrived as if by magic among them nymphaea and watercress. So did the blanket weed when the sun started to warm the water. There was so much to begin with that I had to haul out armfuls of this soft green hair-like substance. By diligently removing it, aerating the water and planting more oxygenators, we kept it more or less under control. Spring fed, the water is glass clear.

The top pond

Fountain magic

Child's play in the top pond

The Top Pond

With ponds, as I see it, there are three choices. One is to have a really small easily managed pond which will attract a surprising amount of wildlife. The second is to have a large managed pond, a lot of work, but fun if you like that sort of thing. The third is to have an unmanaged wild pond, bordered with reeds and rushes and largely left to itself, preferably in an obscure part of the garden. It will need some clearing from time to time. A friend looked at me and said, "But what about the mosquitoes?" I replied that the swallows love them and there are some very effective insect repellents. But she won't have a pond.

The Bog Garden

The rockery, which falls away from the top pond, ends up in a wide shallow ditch created by a water pipe, which crosses the garden encased in concrete, now covered with moss. It makes a perfect damp garden for such thirsty feeders as rodgersias, trollius and variegated *Iris pseudacorus*. In the spring, brunnera and different varieties of kingcups complement each other. The

Huge rogersias in the bog garden

kingcup theme follows down the garden through all the ponds at this time of the year. Crocosmia seems happy too, but where is it not happy? I have seen it clinging to Cornish cliffs and growing in woods. The water drains away into the middle pond, and the bed never becomes really waterlogged and even narcissus seem quite happy. The garden here also supports two varieties of the often misnamed arum lily *Zantendeschia aethiopica*. They are 'Crowborough' and one I brought home from Madeira, 'Green Goddess'. They are perfectly hardy, making beautiful cut flowers and give the garden an exotic air. This damp place is a perfect home for frogs, toads, newts and the occasional grass snake. No wonder there are no slugs. I've learned to live with all these wild things, and can even pick up the odd mouse that the cat brings in. Not sure about the grass snake.

Brilliant euphorbia. Orange in the border can be tricky but here it blends with the brilliant colours of the rock roses

Iris ensalata *'Reveille' in the bog garden with rodgersias*

The bog garden

*Opposite: Trollius, an escapee
from Cumbria but happy here*

*White astilbe flowers from July
onwards and fades gracefully*

The Middle Pond

The middle pond is in the care of my neighbour and has some interesting plants in the shallow end, among them pickerel weed or pontaderia with its tall lance shaped leaves, and skunk cabbage, lysichitum. Water hawthorn *Raponogyton distachyos* adorns the surface for most of the year.

The middle pond lies at the lower level and needs to be drained annually to remove leaves. The caltha are happy in the residual mud and repeat their brilliance down the garden. Spring fed, the pond soon refills.

Water hawthorn Aponogeton
distachyus *grows in the shady
deep end of this pond, blooming
twice a year.   A treasure.*

*A heron glides slowly down to the
shore to fish from the jetty*

*Finally the bottom pond leads to the lake
shore and a view of the fen beyond*

*Golden ginkgo, larch burning red, and dark
green vibernum already full of flowers,
all reflected in the water*

The bottom pond in autumn

The Bottom Pond

The bottom pond is deeper and, being under trees, attracts no blanket weed, but it does need to be dredged at one end each year to keep it healthy. It supports curly pondweed, cover for the many small perch and rudd which inhabit it. Freshwater mussels too. Early on in my management of it, a green algae turned it into pea soup. I had, however, been told that a farmer with a similar problem, had accidentally dropped a bale of barley straw into his pond and it had completely cleared. I did likewise and in a couple of weeks the water was glass clear. My only problem was to remove the bale, now soaked with water and disintegrating fast. I believe that now it is possible to buy it in small packs!

The Lake Shore

When we came here in 1985, the lake was almost inaccessible, due to the fallen trees and an excess of reeds and rushes. We made a small gravelled beach,

The lake shore in 1984

...and a little later

The shingle beach

The leat flowing into the lake

Primula japonica *along the leat*

bordering a wide grass path, but were careful to leave all the wild iris, meadowsweet and big areas of reeds in the lake for the nesting birds, coot, moorhen and mallard.

We directed the water flowing from the bottom pond into a leat which drains into the lake via a boggy area planted with *Primula japonica* and *Primula florindii*. Further along the waterside I planted kingcups, *Caltha palustris*, and at the other end of the beach, astilbes, *Zantendeschia aethiopica* 'Crowborough'. Water forget-me-knots, purple loosestrife and meadowsweet appeared and thrived in the peaty soil. I hope dear Dr Beverley would have approved.

Wild iris

"And lo, the shining levels of the lake" Polygonum campanulatum
is a good companion plant with purple loosestrife

The Front Garden

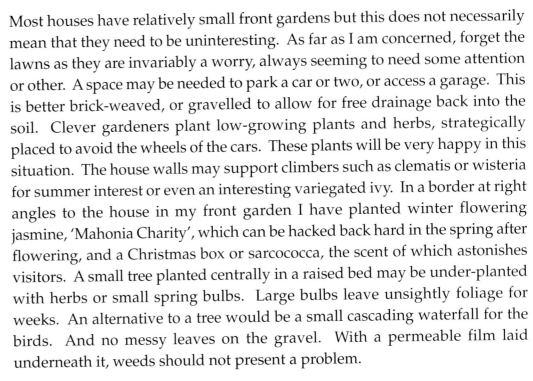

Most houses have relatively small front gardens but this does not necessarily mean that they need to be uninteresting. As far as I am concerned, forget the lawns as they are invariably a worry, always seeming to need some attention or other. A space may be needed to park a car or two, or access a garage. This is better brick-weaved, or gravelled to allow for free drainage back into the soil. Clever gardeners plant low-growing plants and herbs, strategically placed to avoid the wheels of the cars. These plants will be very happy in this situation. The house walls may support climbers such as clematis or wisteria for summer interest or even an interesting variegated ivy. In a border at right angles to the house in my front garden I have planted winter flowering jasmine, 'Mahonia Charity', which can be hacked back hard in the spring after flowering, and a Christmas box or sarcococca, the scent of which astonishes visitors. A small tree planted centrally in a raised bed may be under-planted with herbs or small spring bulbs. Large bulbs leave unsightly foliage for weeks. An alternative to a tree would be a small cascading waterfall for the birds. And no messy leaves on the gravel. With a permeable film laid underneath it, weeds should not present a problem.

Opposite and overleaf: A small rockery at the front of the house welcomes visitors with hellebores and heathers in February and lathyrus and erythroniums in April

The planting at the front of the now well-dressed house leads straight into the garden

New Projects

Nearly every year I embark on some new project in the garden, always, however, designed to incur a minimum of work. The area of gravel above the lakeshore is lined with the permeable film originally put there to deter weeds. It was planted with a variety of cytisus or broom, which has finally succumbed to old age. I planted various small clumps of coloured grasses; blue, green, brown and gold, and a giant stipa. Silhouetted against the lake in the sun, their fragile stems look quite magical. Nepeta or catmint, agapanthus, eryngium, and a scotch thistle or two for height and a bit of drama complete the picture; well, until I add a few more. Few weeds pierce the permeable film.

The grass garden

Eryngium 'Miss Willmot's Ghost' happy in a gravel garden

Opposite: Crocus tomasinianus

A bee-friendly border

Another eventually successful project was the wild flower meadow on the south-west border of the garden. I had cut down one yew tree and reduced another. I had not realised that these trees still carried Protection Orders and the District Council sued me and it ended with a bill of £8,000. Considering all the tree planting I had done when designing the layout of the cemetery, and elsewhere in the village, many people thought this was a bit harsh. Although at one time we had considered submitting a planning application for a family bungalow on this site, which would have been in line with the houses in Postwick Lane, this was in fact never done. As required we replaced the felled yew, planted well away from the now very tall walnut, which it had been smothering and planted fruit trees. I decided to turn the area into a wild flower meadow with mown paths between the fruit trees. Small wild narcissus bloom in March and from then on the grass grows freely until cut down in early autumn. The fruit trees are generously mulched in spring and pruned if necessary in winter; a trouble free, and productive part of the garden.

The orchard

*The walnut tree before
the squirrels raided it*

Saving Work

Opposite, clockwise from top left: These lilies never leave their pots and bloom every year. A tub of penstemon and one of lilies give summer glamour. Even more glamour with brugmansia

I open the door, and there is always something new to see

It is a well known fact that many people, otherwise content with their homes, feel the need to move because they are finding the garden unmanageable. I have therefore collected together my suggestions for reducing the work. Not all of them, or course, will apply to everyone, but some may be helpful, and over the years I have had to take my own advice, sometimes against my inclination towards perfect.

Aims

So let us first consider what one wants from a garden, and how it might best be achieved. I suppose that in Britain more time is spent looking at the garden from inside than is actually spent out in it. The view from the windows, therefore, is quite important and might be the first consideration when re-thinking the lay-out. A garden is a place for growing and enjoying beautiful plants and I sometimes think that too much time is spent thinking about the work and too little time actually looking at it. We should always have time to examine the minute and intricate details of the flowers that we grow. When you step into your garden from your house, you should be able to sit down and look at it. These days many more gardens have a paved area near the house because eating outside and socialising has become increasingly popular. This area might be enlarged, and does not have to be a riot of work-intensive pots. A few well chosen perennials will do, possible climbing up the house.

Seating

Apart from those on the patio or terrace, I consider the location of seats in the garden absolutely vital, and find that there are rarely enough places to sit down. Landscaping places to accommodate permanent benches or chairs creates interest as well as convenience. These places may be paved or more cheaply gravelled, and each area becomes a garden within a garden. Shrubs, ivy-covered trellis, wattle fencing or a rose-arch may be used for shelter or whatever may be appropriate. Do have permanent seats in your garden. You will sit in it far more often than if chairs have to be hauled out of the back of the shed on the odd rare warm day in February, and maybe those days are becoming less rare. I have found that the easiest form of mobile seating is to fit a board hinged to the handles of a roller-ball wheelbarrow. I made one for my mother when she was gardening in her late eighties.

Rosa 'White Cloud'

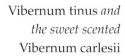

Vibernum tinus *and*
the sweet scented
Vibernum carlesii

There are many varieties of
ceanothus, one I chose was
'Puget Blue'

Ceanothus 'Yankee Point'

Magnolia soulangeana

Silver and gold euonymous is evergreen and colourful

Opposite: Variegated philadelphus growing with Pieris forestii

Rhus typhina - *the Stagshorn Sumach in autumn*

Finally the Cost

To landscape even a small garden all at once with seating areas and a variety of beds planted with trees, shrubs, bulbs and ground-covering plants would be quite an expensive undertaking. Very expensive if it were to include walls, brick-weave paths and water features. Re-arranging it, however, over a period of time whilst cutting down on the maintenance, need not be too daunting. Money spent on growing seeds and saving the all inclusive cost of lawn maintenance will buy quite a number of shrubs. Many, indeed most of my plants, have been acquired from friends and plant sales. So from now on if you have decided to join the brigade of low maintenance gardeners, cross off fungicides, pesticides, fertilizers and composts from your shopping list. The only chemicals I use are weed killers on the gravel paths. Used with care they really do cut down the work.

Crocosmia along a grass path

Cornus kousa *'chinensis' creates a great show in the shrub border in summer*

*Gravel or chipped bark paths complement
the borders and are a vital ingredient
of the landscaping in an informal garden*

Chipped bark through the woods

In Conclusion

I hope some of the suggestions included here have been helpful. Gardeners are an innovative breed. They also tend to be obsessive. When once they accept the idea of reducing work without reducing the pleasure that the garden brings, they cannot fail to succeed.

I should never have had the confidence to take on the restoration and re-landscaping of Brundall Gardens if I hadn't had the experience of caring for many different gardens during my gardening life. When I founded the Broadland Flower Club, I met many flower arrangers who were also keen gardeners and we swapped plants and knowledge. We realised that plants that complimented each other in a flower arrangement would probably do so in the garden. My passion for plant associations developed, and it shows in the garden.

I was invited to become a member of the Norfolk and Norwich Horticultural Society Committee and in the company of real experts was introduced to many new plants.

Cowslips growing wild

I have been opening Brundall Gardens to the public now under the National Gardens Scheme for twenty-seven years, and during that time have met many thousands of gardeners. And what a varied group of people we are. Gardening means different things to different people. Some are perfectionists competing for prizes at shows; others regard the garden as an outdoor living space or play area for children. To others it is a trust for the care of the environment. I have been a member of the Norfolk Wildlife Trust, The Broads Society and Plant Heritage for many years and endeavour to keep Brundall Gardens as the wildlife paradise it should be. I hope that our successors will do likewise.

🌸 Opening Your Garden

Since 1927 an ever increasing number of people have been inviting visitors into their gardens to raise money for nursing charities. Originally it was for retired nurses with no pension, but now it is for specialist nursing, for patients with cancer, the Macmillan and Marie Curie nurses.

Initially the idea of inviting strangers into their gardens is, to many, a terrifying thought, but when you see your bulbs blossoming under the flowering trees you might wish to share the magic of your garden with your friends and neighbours.

Some garden openers do, of course, make a great performance of it and enjoy the incentive it gives them to mow and edge and weed as never before. Others like to show off a collection of prize-winning flowers or vegetables and enjoy the admiring looks they inspire. And if you have got it flaunt it! But if you are a gardener, having another gardener to talk to about your plot be they old or young, rich or poor, experienced or not, is great fun.

And in 25 years of opening my garden I have never known anyone leave litter or steal so much as a cutting, well not when I was looking anyway. Whilst rescuing my garden it has helped to raise thousands of pounds for many charities, but mainly for the National Gardens Scheme.

So if you have a lovely garden call the NGS to discuss opening it. When it is as its best. There is help at hand.